CONCORD BRANCH LIBRARY
2900 SALVIO STREET
CONCORD, CALIFORNIA 94519

CONCORD

SEP 1 6 2003

D0459108

People in My Community

Dentist

CONTRA COSTA COUNTY LIBRARY   WITHDRAWN

by Jacqueline Laks Gorman
Photographs by Gregg Andersen

Reading consultant: Susan Nations, M.Ed., author/literacy coach/consultant

WEEKLY **WR** READER®
EARLY LEARNING LIBRARY

3 1901 03321 6112

Please visit our web site at: **www.earlyliteracy.cc**
For a free color catalog describing Weekly Reader® Early Learning Library's
list of high-quality books, call 1-877-445-5824 (USA) or 1-800-387-3178 (Canada).
Weekly Reader® Early Learning Library's fax: (414) 336-0164.

Library of Congress Cataloging-in-Publication Data

Gorman, Jacqueline Laks, 1955-
    Dentist / by Jacqueline Laks Gorman.
      p. cm. — (People in my community)
    Summary: Photographs and simple text introduce the work done by
a dentist.
    Includes bibliographical references and index.
    ISBN 0-8368-3293-0 (lib. bdg.)
    ISBN 0-8368-3300-7 (softcover)
    1. Dentistry—Juvenile literature. 2. Children—Preparation for dental
care—Juvenile literature. [1. Dentists. 2. Occupations.] I. Title.
RK63.G67   2002
617.6—dc21   2002023887

This edition first published in 2002 by
Weekly Reader® Early Learning Library
330 West Olive Street, Suite 100
Milwaukee, WI 53212 USA

Copyright © 2002 by Weekly Reader® Early Learning Library

Art direction and page layout: Tammy Gruenewald
Photographer: Gregg Andersen
Editorial assistant: Diane Laska-Swanke
Production: Susan Ashley

All rights reserved. No part of this book may be reproduced, stored in a retrieval system,
or transmitted in any form or by any means, electronic, mechanical, photocopying, recording,
or otherwise without the prior written permission of the copyright holder.

Printed in the United States of America

1 2 3 4 5 6 7 8 9 06 05 04 03 02

Note to Educators and Parents

Reading is such an exciting adventure for young children! They are beginning to integrate their oral language skills with written language. To encourage children along the path to early literacy, books must be colorful, engaging, and interesting; they should invite the young reader to explore both the print and the pictures.

People in My Community is a new series designed to help children read about the world around them. In each book young readers will learn interesting facts about some familiar community helpers.

Each book is specially designed to support the young reader in the reading process. The familiar topics are appealing to young children and invite them to read — and re-read — again and again. The full-color photographs and enhanced text further support the student during the reading process.

In addition to serving as wonderful picture books in schools, libraries, homes, and other places where children learn to love reading, these books are specifically intended to be read within an instructional guided reading group. This small group setting allows beginning readers to work with a fluent adult model as they make meaning from the text. After children develop fluency with the text and content, the book can be read independently. Children and adults alike will find these books supportive, engaging, and fun!

— Susan Nations, M.Ed., author, literacy coach, and consultant in literacy development

The dentist has
an important job.
The dentist takes
care of people.

5

The dentist takes care of your mouth. The dentist takes care of your teeth.

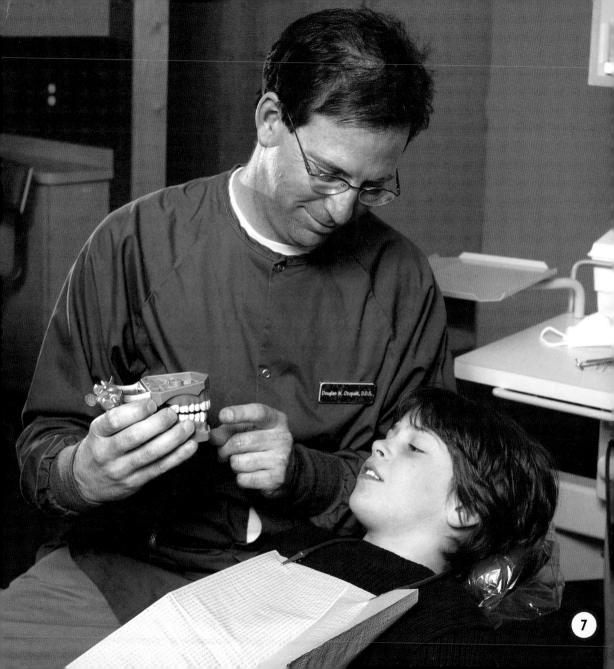

The dentist uses special tools. He shines a bright light in your mouth.

The dentist looks at your teeth with a **mirror**. She checks your teeth with a tool called an **explorer**.

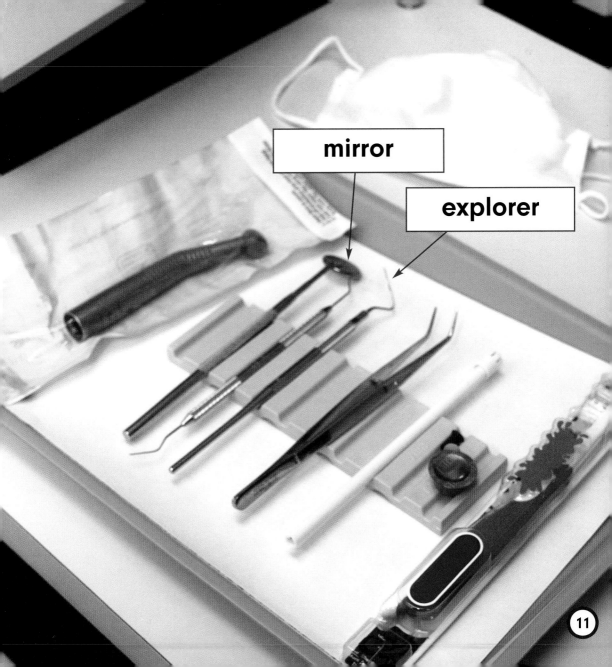

mirror

explorer

The dentist cleans your teeth. She shows you how to brush your teeth with a **toothbrush**.

toothbrush

Sometimes the dentist takes **X-ray pictures** of your teeth with an X-ray machine.

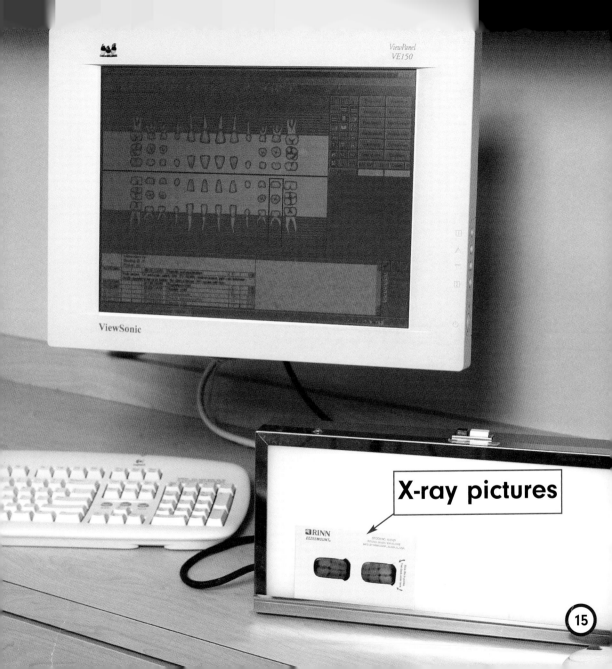

X-ray pictures

The dentist makes you feel better if you have a toothache.

You should visit the dentist two times a year. This keeps your teeth healthy.

It looks like fun
to be a dentist.
Would you like
to be a dentist
some day?

Glossary

dentist — a doctor who takes care of your teeth

explorer — a tool that dentists use to check and clean teeth

mirror — a surface that reflects something

toothache — a pain in a tooth

toothbrush — a tool that you use to clean your teeth

For More Information

Fiction Books

Berenstain, Stan and Jan. *The Berenstain Bears Visit the Dentist.* New York: Random House, 1981.

Brown, Marc. *Arthur Tricks the Tooth Fairy.* New York: Random House, 1997.

Nonfiction Books

Ready, Dee. *Dentists.* Mankato, Minn.: Bridgestone Books, 1998.

Schaefer, Lola M. *We Need Dentists.* Mankato, Minn.: Pebble Books, 2000.

Web Sites

ADA Kids' Corner

www.ada.org/public/topics/kids/index.html

Games and answers to questions about dental health

Going to the Dentist

www.kidshealth.org/kid/feel_better/people/go_dentist.html

What happens at the dentist's office

Index

About the Author

Jacqueline Laks Gorman is a writer and editor. She grew up in New York City and began her career working on encyclopedias and other reference books. Since then, she has worked on many different kinds of books. She lives with her husband and children, Colin and Caitlin, in DeKalb, Illinois.